this book belong to

n. molesworth

St Custards

England

Europe

The World

The universe Space

XY3
π

XYZ

2 634 785

316?

216

13,000
130 00

13
6
98
110
188 = x

6²
1
63
1
67
1
65

6386 512
1636 521
767636 1
0130100
000000
100000
000000
111111

BOTENY STINKS

54321½
5

76783
15415
521 90

HOW TO BE TOPP

Sir Molesworth

How To Be Topp

A guide to Sukcess for
tiny pupils, including
all there is to kno about

SPACE

Geoffrey Willans
and
Ronald Searle

PAVILION

This edition first published in Great Britain in 1992 by
PAVILION BOOKS LIMITED
196 Shaftesbury Avenue, London WC2H 8JL
Copyright © Geoffrey Willans and Ronald Searle 1954

The moral right of the author has been asserted.

Cover designed by Bet Ayer

A CIP catalogue record for this book
is available from the British Library.

ISBN 1 85145 9650

Printed and bound in Great Britain by Clays Ltd

2 4 6 8 10 9 7 5 3

This book may be ordered by post
direct from the publisher. Please contact
the Marketing Department.
But try your bookshop first.

Molesworth ography

In 1951, about the time I had decided to abandon drawing St Trinian's, D.B. Wyndham Lewis – always ready to stick his neck out – suggested that we should collaborate on a St Trinian's romance. His *alter ego* 'Timothy Shy' would write a story if I would agree to do the pictures. I decided to have this last fling and made the drawings, which confirmed to me that I was sick to death of the subject.

The Terror of St Trinian's appeared in October 1952. By Christmas it had sold around 45,000 copies, and Max Parrish, its publisher, urged us to follow up the success at once with a sequel. Wyndham Lewis was keen, but not me, and I refused.

To cheer up a despondent Max, I rashly promised that he should have a better best-seller for the following Christmas. The promise was kept.

Shortly before my meeting with Max Parrish, a journalist friend, Geoffrey Willans, then working with the BBC European Service, had asked whether I could help him put together – and even find a publisher for – a book about schoolboys (groan). Geoffrey had written an occasional series for *Punch* in the Forties, based on his experiences as a school teacher. It was written through the myopic eyes of one Nigel Molesworth, later known as 'the curse of St Custards'.

What Geoffrey had given me to read I finally got round to reading and (surprise) I thought it madly funny. With Max Parrish in mind we set about shaping the idea into a book and I took the result to Max. He wasn't exactly overwhelmed, but finally agreed to take it on for an advance of £300 between Geoffrey and myself, provided I would illustrate the text as 'profusely' as I had the St Trinian's book.

In less time than it takes to produce a baby, *Down With Skool* appeared, and between October and Christmas 1953 had sold 53,848 copies. The saga of The Curse of St Custards was away.

Before Geoffrey died of a heart attack in August 1958, at the ridiculously young age of 47, an anthology – *The Compleet Molesworth* – was already in proof, comprising by then three best-selling volumes and most of a fourth to come the following year – *Back in the Jug Agane*.

Like *The Compleet Molesworth*, *Back in the Jug Agane* was published after Geoffrey's death. Molesworth joined St Trinian's on the Elysian playing fields and that was the end of school(girl or boy) drawings for me.

Sad that Geoffrey is not around to see the phoenix arise after a quarter of a century of hibernation ect ect chiz moan drone. But whilst he lingers up there in Universt Space (hello clouds hello sky) Nigel is his worthy spokesperson AS YOU WILL SEE. Nowe read on . . .

Ronald Searle

Contents

CONTENTS

Cave !

You kno who this is e.g. Me nigel molesworth the curse of st custard's. I can't be a sec becos they hav got me on the run and all the headmasters in britain are after me with their GATS and COSHES ect. I kno what it means when they catch up tho actually headmasters seldom do they are fat and canot run for tooffe.

At the moment I am using the natural history museum as a hideout. My friend peason sa i shall be safe there as they will not tell me from all the newts stoats bats and tiny crawling creatures they hav there chiz.

Anyway there is just time to give my felow suferers the fruits of my xperience. You could becom topp if you want to but most pupils do not. If they use this book they could come half way up or even botom hem-hem. Hist! A noise! If they get me before long this will help to cary on the good work. i confess it was me who pinched the cheese from the matron's mousetrap. Hard cheese on the mouse ha-ha. It was me who—

Blud · · Blud

1

BACK TO SKOOL AGANE!

This is wot it is like when we go back on the skool trane. There are lots of new bugs and all there maters blub they hav every reason if they knew what they were going to. For us old lags however it is just another stretch same as any other and no remision for good conduc. We kno what it will be like at the other end Headmaster beaming skool bus ratle off leaving trail of tuck boxes peason smugling in a box of flat 50 cigs fotherington-tomas left in the lugage rack and new bugs stand as if amazed. Skool now smell not only of chalk latin books skool ink foopball boots and birdseed but carbolic soap as well. White jugs stand in rows in the dorms and various weeds are about the place looking unaturaly clean and civilised. Who knows what adventures in work and pla the next term will bring forth. And who cares, eh?

2

HOW TO SUCCEED AS
A NEW BUG

New bugs are wets and weeds their mummies blub when they kiss them goodby while seniors such as me hem-hem stand grimly by licking their slobering chops. No more dolies or William the bear to cuddle and hug, no more fairy stories at nanny's knee it is all aboard the fairy bus for the dungeons. You hav to hav a bit of patience but once the trane moves out the little victims are YOURS. You put them in the lugage rack with molesworth 2.

Paters at the moment are patting the blubing maters.

'It is all right old gurl,' they sa. 'Skools are not wot they were in my day. Boys are no longer cruel to each other and the masters are frends.'

'But my Eustace hav been taken away. He is only a baby.'

(*You are dead right he is. Fancy sending him to skool with a name like Eustace. They deserve it all.*)

Pater stare at his glass of gin reflectively. It will be peaceful at home now. He can relax at the weekends and if it is a good skool Eustace will soon be strong and brany enuff to bring in the coal. He sa:

'Now in my day it was diferent. When i first went to Grunts they tosted me on a slo fire. Then i ran the gauntlet being flicked with wet towels. Then they stood me aganst the mantelpeace as i am standing now—'

BANG! CRASH!

12

Mater gives him sharp uper cut folowed by right cross then zoom up to bed leaving pater wondering why women are so unpredictable. Glumly he pours himself another gin.

MEANWHILE AT ST CUSTARDS . . . . . .

Eustace hav been trussed to a chair and a pair of socks are stuffed in his mouth to stifle his desperate cries. 'Now,' sa molesworth the Pukon 'we will submit you to three trillion volts of the nuclear torturer.' . . .

DOWN BELOW IN THE STUDY . . . . . .

Tinkle, tinkle.

Is that the telephone, my dere?

Nothing else go tinkle, tinkle, swetehart, unless it be the photograph of that repulsive old custardian in its brite silver frame. Shall I answer?

Pray do.

Tinkle, tink—

It is mrs togglington to enquire after Eustace. Oh yes he hav setled down very well. He was as quiet and as good as a lamb.

(*Thinks: Which one was he?*)

Yes, there is no need to wory. He hav no spots his head do not ache his knok knees hav given him no trouble. He is as far as we kno unlikely to develop a disease tonite. He hav changed his socks and cleaned his fangs. I have put him in the charge of a v. reliable boy e.g. dere little nigel molesworth.

Eustace mater ring off very relieved cheers cheers and telephone all the other lades about it. Headmaster and wife continue to make wool rug. Masters shiver in their cells. An owl hoot and Eustace is insensible. St custard's hav begun another term.

TEKNEEK FOR NEW BUGS

HOW NOT TO SUCCEED

New bug is lying back in best chair in the library in portion of the room reserved for prefects. He is eating sweets. Head of the skool enters who hav been chosen for his qualities of leadership devotion to st custard's ect. In other words he is grabber and joly tuough.

GRABBER: You hav a face like a flea and you could not lift a cucumber.

new bug (with a yawn): Tu quoque, oaf. You also hav a face like a flea and could not lift wot the french call a concombre.

GRABBER: Do you kno who you are talking to?

new bug: Can it be stalin?

GRABBER: i am head of the skool captin of games martial of the squash courts custodian of shooting and garter principal of the natural history museum.

new bug: So what? i am not impressed by wot I hav seen around here. The old brigade hav been in too long. There hav got to be changes. The younger generation is knoking at the door hav some buble gum.

GRABBER: Wot's your name?

new bug: the lord cedric furnival crabthorn percy constance charles plunk. (*He blows a balloon in his buble gum cooly*) you may call me pongo.

(*Exit.*)

SUCCESS

In order to sukceed all new bugs should take a vow of silence for i year. When a senior pass they should lie down and let him walk over them. They should ofer swetes saing go on take the whole bag. They must clean shoes and think of pleasing others. They should not shout molesworth is a grate big wet and then run away to matron.

Aktualy you canot ever get new bugs to behave like that and the best thing is to avoid them. If you get put in charge of them it is like a film of sno white all in technicolour or 3D or something.

> *new bugs are all sitting on toadstools in forest plaing with lambs and deers. Birds flit about. Enter molesworth growling and cursing.*

come here you horrid ticks!

(*All cower the forest goes dark.*)

do you hear me ticks. You will all get six!
A robin: tweet!
who said that? i will bash the lot of you. i will utterly tuough you up.

(*Thunder: all the new bugs deer and lambs run away. Litening pla around my horns.*)

get your handiwork cracking produce your plastissene for free xpresion and the other wedy things you do.

(*i catch a new bug and let him dance on the palm of my hand.*)

a new bug: you are not tuough.
Wot me?
a new bug: you hav a hart of gold.
Discovered! Curses!
a new bug: won't you pla with us?
No!
a new bug: Come on fellers he won't hurt you he is a grate big sham.
All: hee-hee-hee-hee! *They dance back with lambs and robins. The sun come out and i find myself singing a song with them chiz chiz chiz chiz chiz.*

Rake's Progress

1. this is parkinson. I want you to help him settle down.

2. Here is your desk, parkinson.

3. Here are some sums. Let us see if you can add.

4.

5.

6.

7.

8.

New bugs often canot write xcept this way :—

The Space*Ship v

However miss pringle soon lick them into shape. She get out her gat and sa : You may look like a lot of new-born babes in yore first grey shorts but it won't wash with me. I am going to hav it MY way. O.K. let's go. All the gifts of sno-drops, aples sweets and ginger biskits do not alter her iron purpose. Before long a new bug can do in his copy-book

The cate sat on

And finally

The love of the poets is a ting apart

He is now in the same spot as the rest of us he hav to write home on Sunda. You would think that this precious link between skool and our dear ones would be cherished by all boys. In fact, let us face it, boys do not like writing home chiz and for a joly good reason. *There is nothing to sa.* Why? Because the truth is so shoking and unspekable that no parent could stand it on a Monday morning. So we hav to gloss it over as it is no use upseting your mater particularly at brekfast on Monday morning.

New bugs when they start writing leters are inclined to be emotional chiz they are a lot of sissies :—

st. custard's,

Darling mama, darling papa,

i mis you very much. i am lonly. plees kiss my gollywog. never did I apreciate so much the joys and com-
forts of home life. To think that i was rud to grandad
that i scremed when i was told to hav a bath. And how
many times hav i refused to come in and go to bed.
O woe. Kiss my gollywog agane.

Yours fathefuly

binkie.

nb you had beter kiss grandad too. Or not. As you plese.

After a bit, though, a new bug gets over this sort of stuff.
i mean gollywogs and tedy bears, I ask you! i would not be
suprised if som of them hav not a doll which say Mama
Mama and go to slepe. Aktualy some toys are not bad. i
had a super monkey called spinach of whom (grammer) i
was very fond. i would always go to slepe with it nestling
on my pilow and . . . . CHIZ! CURSES!
wot am i saying?

Leters home in the end develop into a contest between
parent and weeny one which come into a full crescendo
in middle-life hem-hem as they sa in some of the sunda
papers. Note the cooling of the ardour. O woe agane but
that is the tragedy nb paters and maters we still luv you
reely. Beter than our gollywogs anyway.

LETER :

st. custard's

Sunda.

Dearest Mummy (and Daddy)

We played aganst porridge court on saturday. We lost 9 – o. The film was a western. Will you send me a bakterial gun. They are 6/6 at grabbers.

With love from

Nigel.

ANSER :

Barleywaters.
Clotshire.

Monda

My dearest darling most beloved nigel,

It was marvelous super to get your lovely long leter with all its news. I have telephoned grabbers to send the gun. *Are you taking your lozenges?* Please let me kno. Wot a shame about porridge court i xpect you will win next year. [hem-hem. not a hope]. There is very litle to tell you. the snodrops are out and yore father is in a filthy temper but these facts hav nothing to do with each other. Do not forget, darling, to let me kno about the lozenges

Your fondest superest ever-loving

Mummy.

P.S. *Don't* forget about the lozenges, darling.

LETER:

> st. custard's.
>
> Sunda.

Dear Mummy and Daddy,

We played aganst howler house on Saturday. We lost 9 – o. The film was micky mouse. Thank you for the bakterial gun. Will you send me a jet-propeled airship. (17/6)

> Love from
> nigel.

ANSER:

> Barleywaters, Clotshire.

My ever-darlingest superest most smashing and admired son Nigel,

Your letter was a wonderful surprise and so full of news. Your handriting hav improved beyond mesure. *You did not mention about the lozenges darling will you be sure and let me kno next time.* Do not wory too much about your lessons i kno you are doing your best. The crocus are out now but yore father is still in a filthy temper so i hav ordered the jet-propeled airship myself. Don't forget about the lozenges and Gollywog send his love.

> Your most tremendously affectionate divinely superly adoring mater

> Mummy

p.s don't forget about the lozenges.

LETER :

st. custard's

Sunda.

Mummy,

(A) v poopwell hall. Lost 6 – o.

(B) tarzan of the apes.

(C) a self-propelling car (£125 – o – o.)

Yrs.

nigel.

OTHER CORESPONDENCE

Of course we do not only get leters from our parents. There are leters from gurl friends and the ushual sekretarial mail as hon. sec. of the youth club hem-hem. There are also those leters which you put away hastily after reading the first line. e.g. *Dere molesworth, Yore overdraft facilities are due for review. – or 2/- each way Claptrap. You win o. You lose 4/- prompt setlement will enable us to kepe our books in order.* All of these are a chiz and on the whole no good comes of them. let us pass to more siggnificant things.

FOR THE TINIES

Some new bugs are so well educcated at their dame skools that they can read when they get to st custards. They will soon forget after a term or 2 give them time give them time. Meanwhile their ever-loving parents send them maggazines and storybooks every thursday chiz to keep alite the dying flame of kulture.

THE WAR-BLER

EV-ERY
MON-DAY

6d

The hap-py mag-a-zine for boys and girls

Price 6d. Published by grabber and grabber, who would luv to give it away to the tinies. Indeed they would if it were not that the little ones must learn that it is only by your own eforts that suksess is won in life hem-hem ask old mr grabber.

THE ADVENTURES OF DIPPY-DOPEY

Dippy-Dopey love–s his cat. He br–ings the cat m–ilk. The cat wishes some–thing strong–er. mee-aouw he sa mee-aouw give me a ry–e on the rocks so c–old that it would fr–eeze an esk–i–mo ig–loo. Ver–y well sa Dippy-Dopey i will try be–cos i luv my cat. Dippy-Dopey runs to town on the toy–land trane. He goes to his old friend Trash, who is a dis–rep–u–table li–on. i want a rye–on–the–rocks for the cat cry Dippy-Dopey. Growl sa Trash i will fix that id–le fo–ol good and pro–per. He k–nock up a white–e lad–y in a jif–fy. Dippy-Dopey run back into the woods with the liq–uid. Where you been sa the cat where you been pour me out a slug quick–ly. He drinks it back. He drinks a–noth–er. And a–noth–er. Now we can go to sleep sa Dippy-Dopey.

St Custard's Explaned

A small experiment in piktorial education for clots who don't kno about it.   Designed and produced by n. molesworth

1. The peason-molesworth space ship threatened by wild mercurian maths masters lies disabled in the onion bed of the kitchen garden.

2. Meanwhile in the master's common room. Sigismund arbuthnot the mad maths master musters his rhomboids.

3. Time off for tea and seed cake. That is peason on the left he is not bad he is my grate friend. My bro molesworth 2 is eating cake as per ushual he is uterly wet and a weed. The other one is me Captain molesworth the interplanetary clot cheers cheers.

4. A new recruit for the hard-pressed crew. Aktually it is only fotherington-tomas you kno he sa Hullo clouds hullo sky he is a girlie and love the scents and sounds of nature tho the less i smell and hear them the better.

5. Wandsworth the skool dog trots up with the missing fusion percolater in his fatheful jaws.

6. Sigismund looks at us through his all-seeing videoscope. We look at him. Impasse.

7. A new plot.

8. Bound and gagged the crew are led into Divinity class.

9. Divinity lesson.

10. Meanwhile . . .

11. grabber blasts the walls with his cosmic disintegrator. he is head of the skool and a bit dim but we had to give him this part.

12. Escape!

13. The peason-molesworth space ship takes off (more next week if you have the necessessary d's otherwise jane is not bad value).

ALL THERE IS TO KNO ABOUT SPACE

There is very little mistery about Space these days at least not to us boys who hav grown up with it. It is just a lot of planets dotted about the place and if you want the gen about them here it is.

THE MOON: This is rather trippery these days as it is only 239000 miles away. Besides it is rather disappointing when you hav been fired all that distance and spent about six years of your life in a space ship to step out and find a lot of craters and moon canals. Agane there is no air so noone can breathe which make things a bit dificult. On the other hand you can jump three times as high as you can on earth but so can everyone else so there is not much fun in it.

URANUS: This is 1782 million miles away and you hav to pass through a belt of planetoids to get there. It is well worth it when you do but that is rather unlikely in your time becos it would take so long to reach that it would be your grate grand child who would hav the fun i.e. he would be murdered by the PUKON and his TREENS. Agane it seme to be rather a long way to go for that.

MARS: Mars would be all right if it were not for the Martians who are quite beyond the pail. Always fighting always quareling no peace at all for the sound of space pistols, H-bombs, gamma-ray guns, bakterial cannons, Z-destructors and A-integgraters it might be Big skool at st custards in brake. I must sa it would be a bit beter if headmasters zoomed in to take the next lesson in a mini-helicopter like the PUKON do from his space palace but you canot hav everything particularly at skool where you get practically o xcept latin and the kane. It would be nice to get to kno some of martian skoolboys but they are moluscs with gogle eyes who talk in high-pitched squeaks. They goble their mars veg and they are most unsavory they do not wash. Not a bit like us. Or are they hem-hem?

SATURN: You can always recognise Saturn when you zoom towards it at the speed of light. First of all it hav 9 little moons and then three rings. Plunge past these, give it full gravity reaction, ease to half, pick up the first space beacon, turn right at the church, flatten out, blo the space tanks and go in to land . . . . . . CRASH WAM BLAM BUMP so you see it is not so very diferent from landing on the earth. And what is it when you get here? The people my dear are such bores. Very hospitable of course but what do you hav in comon with walking toadstools which is what they are. The rest of them are giant bullfrogs and that is, when you come to think of it, not much beter. They croak and bark. Beter to stay at home really the people at parties there are like bullfrogs and they croak and bark to. But they don't hop out of the window and pinch your space ship. If they pinch anything it's – enuff said hem-hem.

SPACE COMPLANTE: Space is getting a bit congested these days what with all the daring space aces who come out every Friday price 4d. It makes it a bit dificult to get a decent adventure the PUKON is taken up with one VORA with another. You try the vilaninous SHAZAM. Zoosh- Zee-Zeeeeee. . . . So you want to play it ruff, Shazam eh: but he sa go away chiz i am planing to invade mercury with a milion trilion space transports. All the fatheful chaps from other planets who hav names like KONX and carvel and faces it is hard to describe hav disapeared along with the saturnians and mercurians who are fortifying their uranium cities. In fact they are all so taken up with xplosions and zooming about that they hav no time for you. Even when you blast them with your gamma-ray pistol – *ziff-ziff-ziff-ziff* – they take no notice. So there is only one thing to do – zoosh – and go off home to tuough up molesworth 2.

3

AKQUIRE CULTURE AND KEEP THE BRANE CLEAN

HOW TO BE TOPP IN LATIN

All skools make some sort of show at teaching the pupils things and the headmaster pin up a huge timetable of lessons ect. which make the heart sink when you look at it. I mean do the grate british nation understand that thousands of its young elizabthans are looking at latin ugh before there brekfast hav even settled. i mean to sa how would they like saing monerer monereris moneretur ect. at that hour eh?

Actually it is quite easy to be topp in lat. you just have to work chiz chiz chiz. Otherwise, there are various ways of taking your mind from it such as altering shorter latin primer into shortbread eating primer and if my name you wish to see turn to page one hundred and three. After that you just stare gloomily at stems in labials form Nom and hope for the best.

The only best that can hapen is when the BELL ring cheers cheers cheers and you can stop puting blotch paper into the inkwell.

Meanwhile lat. master drones on. He is always frightfully keen on lat. which he call classicks amo amas amat gender rhymes bonus and hic haec hoc which he quote with glee. Fancy a grown man saying hujus hujus hujus as if he were proud of it it is not english and do not make SENSE.

Lat. masters are always convinced that lat. is easy quite pappy. They encourage you. It is so *simple* molesworth they cry if you will only try.

Now go at it quite calmly.

Tandem novum quidem et inauditum consilium capit . . .

Simple eh hav a hart like all lat. it is just all BOSH.
Sometimes they think they will trick you into liking lat.
by having a latin pla. Latin plas are like this –

THE HOGWARTS

by

MARCUS PLAUTUS MOLESWORTHUS

Sene One. The villa of Cotta at Rome. Enter CORTICUS a
  dreary old slave and RADIX his mate.

CORTICUS: (*laying a skin of wine on the sideboard*) Eheu!
  (The headmaster and all lat. masters who watch roar
  with larffter.)

RADIX: Eheu!
  (*More larffter they are in stitches*)

CORTICUS: Eheu!

RADIX: Eheu!
  (*The curtain falls as the masters roll helplessly in the
  aisles.*)

Sene Two. A tavern off the Via apia. Enter MENSA a dirty old man followed by ANNUS his shieldbearer.

MENSA: Tot quot, clot.

ANNUS: Tu quoque, clotie.

> (They trip over each other's togas. An ancient Briton enters in chains.)

BRITON: Turn it up now turn it up.

> (*The curtain falls with all masters in hysterics.*)

Sene Three: The Capitol. Cotta and his wife are at breakfast.

COTTA: Quid est pabulum?

WIFE: (*handing the cornflakes*) Vis.

COTTA: Eheu!

> *IDIOTICUS their son enters singing to the lyre.*

IDIOTICUS: To nouns that canot be declined
   The neuter gender is assigned.
   Bebop bebop
   Examples fas and nefas give
   And the Verb-Noun Infinitiv.

> (*This is too much for the masters who join rolicking in the chorus. The geese begin to quack and all the actors forget their lines. Curtain.*)

MOLESWORTH V MORON & MORON
(*peason intervening*)

If you do not partikularly care a buton if you are topp or not, one of the best things is to get into a DISCUSSION about it (in English). Like this. You put aside your dabcriket (hutton 2002) and look v. puzzled and with a thirst for knoledge.

Sir?

Be quiet molesworth! Get on with your exercise.

No sir really sir.

Well, what is it? (Thinks: A possible trap?)

Then you sa:

What is the *use* of latin sir?

Master clutches the board ruber but he knos he is beaten this one always rouses the mob. The class breaks into an uproar with boos catcalls and cries of 'Answer!' The master begin

er well er that er quite simple molesworth. latin is er classicks you kno and classicks are – well they are er – they are the studies of the ancient peoples.

SIR NIGEL MOLESWORTH Q.C. So what?

er latin gives you not only the history of Rome but er (*hapy inspiration*) its culture, it er tells you about interesting men like J. Caesar, hannibal, livy, Romulus remus and er lars porsena of clusium.

SIR NIGEL MOLESWORTH, Q.C. And the Gauls you do not mention the Gauls. Would you not consider them interesting.

O most certainly.

SIR NIGEL MOLESWORTH Q.C. (*consulting his brief*) I observe from the work of this class that the Gauls hav atacked the camp with shouts they hav frightened the citizens, they hav killed the enemy with darts and arows and blamed the belgians. They hav also continued to march into Italy. Would it not be more interesting if they did something new?

er possibly.

SIR NIGEL MOLESWORTH Q.C. Would you perhaps explane why latin never deals with the exploits of nero and one or two of the fruitier emperors. Or empresses for that mater?

(*The master is silent clutching the board ruber convulsilvely. Sir Nigel looks round the court with a meaning look*)

That is my case, m'lud.

(*He sits down on the inkwell which peason hav shoved under him.*)

That is my case, m'lud

Aktually it never really hapens like that. You hav to listen to the same old stuff about latin giving you depth and background. It is also the base of english words but it canot be base enuff for me chiz.

Another wizard wheeze is to look up something really tricky in the grammer e.g. gerunds which are always tricky and shifty if you ever get as far as looking at them. What hapens is as follows:

Hand up (*Silence for 5 minits*)

Sir (*whisper no repli*)

Hand up agane. (*3 minits two secs.*)

What is it, molesworth?

Sir, what is a gerund? (*Master stare at you as if amazed*)

What is what? (He hav never heard of it)

A gerund, sir.

You ought to kno that. Look it up, boy. (*working himself into a rage*) really the ignorance of 2B they are the worst form i hav ever taken. What is a gerund, indeed! Worse than 3A last year! Much worse.

But what *is* a gerund, sir?

I hav told you look it up look it up look it up. (*turning the leaves of the grammer beneath the desk*) A gerund is a – it is a verbal substantive, molesworth, declined like neuters of the second declension any fule knos that. It seems to me extraordinary ect . . . . . .

It is a pity really that you can't cob masters cribbing and get them 6 of the best but there it is. Festina lente as we say to each other lightly at brake. Festina lente or l'll bash you up.

The Private Life of the Gerund

The gerund attacks some peaceful pronouns

Kennedy discovers the gerund and leads it back into captivity

A gerund shut out. No place for it in one of my sentences

Social snobery. A gerund 'cuts' a gerundive

LATIN PROSE

In the end you hav to come face to face with latin and here is the sort of thing that apperes and my coments.

Test. (3 weakly.) Into Latin:

a) *The ramparts of the enemy are long.*
How long that is the point? If we kno how long they are we can march to the end and go round. Otherwise we must bring up the ballista and catapult our men over. In any case why bother me. Labienus is your man third tent on the right. Hand me back my chisel i am writing to mum.

b) *The boy's head is small, his feet are big.*
Ho! He hav also a face like a wild baboon, arms like a flea and a nose like a squished turnip. He is uterly wet and a weed and it is obviously my grate friend peason.

c) *All the cavalry are on the right wing.*
I ask you! they just chase the ball like the ticks in the third game. Look at Caesar. What's he doing there when he ought to be on the left wing eh? Labienus Cotta and Balbus — what a half-back line. *Mark your men!* Get back in gole, Remus! Wot a shambles i ask you no wonder the hungarians beat them.

d) *Do you always carry your books on your head?*
No, not always. Sometimes i carry an iron bar or a basket of washing on it it depends on my mood. What, then, do i do with my books? i deface them tear off the covers thro them at fotherington-tomas churn them about in my desk make blotches on them and make tunels with them for my trains. What business is it of yours anyway?

e) *Does the clear voice of the girl delight your ears?*
i might hav known it.

THE MOLESWORTH DAY-DREAM
SERVICE 1

Are you fatigued? Bored, run-down, depressed? Are Caesar and Labienus too much for you? Do the Gauls want to make you scream?

The answer is simple.

Help yourself to a MOLESWORTH DAY-DREAM. Simple, easy to operate. No gadgets. Just detach yourself from the hum-drum work of the class and stare out of the window with your mouth open.

THE GRATE ST CUSTARD'S FLOOD

Up Up Up the swirling waters rise steadily. The vegetable garden and playing fields are a sea of water old foopball boots float in the skool yard. Inside corridors and classrooms are deep in water. Another pair of foopball boots floats by with molesworth 2 beneath them.

'That proves,' i sa, reeling him in, 'that you are uterly wet.'

In his study the headmaster sits at his desk with the waters rising to his nose.

'What is it?' he sa irritably at my knock.

'Sir the skool is flooded.'

'Go away boy don't worry me report it to the master on duty.'

At this point the waters gurgle into his pipe putting it out with a rore and hiss of steam. The matron, carried by the current, drifts in through the window. She smiles wanly but says nothing.

'What is this molesworth?' sa the headmaster. 'If this is another of your jokes i warn you there may be serious konsequences.'

At that moment a bust of Shakespeare falls upon his head.

'Great Scott!' he exclames. 'What the Dickens is that?'
(Ha-Ha)

Then he give a grate cry: 'My kanes! They are drifting
away.'

Too late the kanes join the swirling jetsam of beetles
prunes sossages protractors bungies masters maps foopballs
and conkers which hav risen like a scum to the surface.
Stuned with his loss headmaster fall insensible.

The galant boys, meanwhile, hav climbed upon floating
blakboards benches and tubs. They punt peacefully across
the skool yard. The chivalrous molesworth hav prudence
entwhistle the beautiful under-matron upon his craft hem-
hem

PRUDENCE: How peaceful it is upon the waters nigel.

ME: (*blushing benethe my boater*) i hav rather a nasty hack
on my shin and can i have a clean handkerchief.

PRUDENCE: Don't let us talk of everyday things nigel. Am
i beautiful

ME: Gosh ur coo i mean to say gosh.

(*We glide benethe the green shade of a willow. There is silence.*)

ME: Prudence –

PRUDENCE: Yes, nigel?

ME: i think on the whole mumps are beter than measles.

(*With a strangled cry she thro the cucumber sandwiches at me.*)

Back at skool the headmaster, recovered, addresses the
survivors.

'It is not my rule,' he sa, 'to grant additional half-hols
during termtime. As the waters are above the ceiling, however, work may stop after this period.'

WOW! WIZZ! CHEERS! SUPER!

WAM! A volume of Livy uneringly thrown strike my
nose. It is followed by a piece of chalk into my open mouth.
That is the worst of dreams. They fade and one must come
back to reality chiz. Quibus quibus quibus but who cares?

Grate Latin Lies

The customs of the Gauls were honourable

Great crimes were rare in ancient times

41

The girls were beautiful

All the Romans love home

4

A FEW MOMENTS IN
THE UNDERWORLD

It is no use sooner or later it has to come you must talk about your felow sufferers e.g. the boys with whom you are forced to mingle. Some are strong others are weedy so it is quite simple.

If boys are strong you sa gosh grabber it was too bad you made a duck at criket it was dashed bad luck you hapned to make a blind swipe and thereby lost the match. The ball was a googly which had you not closed your eyes tight you mite hav seen. (*Tact*)

If a boy is weedier than you it is diferent you sa Look at little baby made a duck little baby couldn't hit a flea. (*Get tuough policy*)

Of course weedy boys always rely on WORDS. e.g. How many did you make last time molesworth?

o

Yar boo sucks l b w i supose the old story i would not swank if i were you after all some are selekted others are not some hav an aptitude for the game others just slog. Slogging never got anyone anywhere.

(This is the time when you spring upon him mightily and proove that criket may be all very well but not very realistic in the modern world where anyone may next moment be going to mars. Xcept of course that mars may hav a joly good team which can make 10002 so boo to huton bedser and all the rest.)

But i digress hem-hem BOYS fall into a lot of types which are all repulsive as i shall make clear.

CADS

Cads hav always a grandmother who is the DUCHESS of BLANK hem hem. They are inclined to cheat at conkers having baked them for 300 years in the ancestral ovens. These conkers belong to the national trust they are so tuough and if you strike one your new conker fly into a 10000000000 bits.* In this case there is nothing to do about it xcept to SMILE.

*The conker was a huge and glossy one like a racehorse, but like all racehorses which are huge and glosy they fall into a ditch so do not back them. They cross their legs and that is never a good thing for a racehorse or a conker.

Back to cads. They sa wot skool are you going to. You sa well it is one of the lesser known publick skools it is called GRUNTS it is in devonshire and my pater thinks that becos it is ok for sons of retired clergymen i will be ok. to eton for you i supose? It is always eton and good luck to them they go to a good show in spite of the fog.

eton is a small paradise in the thames valley. New bugs who arive are met by the maitre d'hotel who sa Welcome sir we have to put you in suite number 2 this is only temporary sir you understand no bathroom no shower your tooth- paste will be waiting for you frozen in the wash-basin.

YOU MUST HAVE PATIENCE. In 3 years you can despise EVERY- BODE the LOT. If you are lucky you can even call the matron a dame which takes a bit of doing. So wot you are still in the thames valley then you can put your shoulder againgst a wall and achive o but less than nothing.

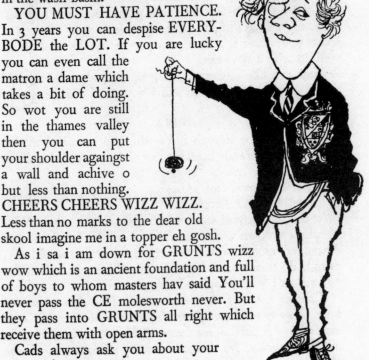

CHEERS CHEERS WIZZ WIZZ. Less than no marks to the dear old skool imagine me in a topper eh gosh.

As i sa i am down for GRUNTS wizz wow which is an ancient foundation and full of boys to whom masters hav said You'll never pass the CE molesworth never. But they pass into GRUNTS all right which receive them with open arms.

Cads always ask you about your pater and mater e.g.

Wot does your pater *do*, molesworth?

Not a stroke positively not a stroke (*a lite larff*)

He is in the city i suppose

Som of the time at other times he is in earls court it depends (*more larffter*)

But what is his job?

You canot get out of this one. There are a lot of jobs for which the younger generation are being trained up to take the places of their fathers. There is a bird seed merchant, skoolmaster, pigeonfancier brassfounder skinner stockbroker and a lot of others in fact it is shoking how many there are. But all of them sound deadly when you sa your pater do them. Like mum you could wish sometimes that your pater was a bit more glamorous but hay ho. The only thing is to jam your monocle in your eye and sa i kno your pater is a lord pauncefoote but he could jolly well do with a new suit.

Then run like the wind. Ho jenkins sponge the mud of the county from my knees and I will stroll into deten.

OIKS

Oiks used to be tuough boys who had not our advantages. Passing us and observing our pink caps and blue noses oiks call out

OO er coo lumme look at them.

Then they buzz a conker.

At this any boy of spirit sa charge ta-ran-ta-ra ta-ran ta-ra cut them down with your swords men. If the whole croc descended upon the oiks how surprised and wot would miss pringle do then poor thing. Aktually this never hapens for odd reason: Miss pringle address us a lecture.

Take no notice of them molesworth. They do not kno any beter. They kno well enough to hit peason on the nose? The old man's beard is thick on the hedges and soon the shy wild violet will be flowering. No molesworth i am not trying to change the subject. Duck! Heads! Oh, what can all this be? Another shower of conkers? Take no notice take no notice. WAM BIFF ur-ur-ur. Keep on the pavement, tinies, do not break ranks. As i was saing the old man's beard is thick upon the — SPLOSH. Keep close this is when your discipline counts. The sqadron must get through and they shall never capture the standard.

And so the oiks behave as they always hav. The trouble is that among any number of oiks there is always a big one called Ern. Ern is a buly. Everyone sa stand up to bulies they will run away but do not believe it. A lot of them stand still and then where are you eh? i will tell you you are in the duck pond and it is joly freezing.

Lately however things are a bit diferent. The oiks have become v. well dressed certainly beter than pauncefootes pater and their skools are quite remarkable with all those windows to let the sunshine in. You only hav to look to see what goes on in there. First the foyer then the palm court lounge and swiming pool and lovely women ect. (Cor crikey ermintrude your pigtails are ropy toda. Can i sip a milk and orange juice with you at the brake.) Well that's what these new places are like and you can pla as long as you like with the skool plutonium plant. Yet our paters and maters shell out to send us to st custards but that is the way it is we just hav to put up with it.

GOODY-GOODIES

There is no beter xsample of a goody-goody than fotherington-tomas in the world in space. You kno he is the one who sa Hullo Clouds Hullo Sky and skip about like a girly. i mean you are just zooming about taking pot shots at various new bugs with your catapult when fotherington-tomas sa Do you think you should be doing that, molesworth, is it kind. Can you not hear the shrieks of agony? To which i repli If i had a germ gun i would blast them with 5 trillion bakterial volts so they are getting off litely. But somehow the plesure has gone.

Goody-goodies believe in fairies father xmas peter pan ect. and unlike most boys they are kind to their sisters. Lots of boys are unfortunate enuff to have weedy sisters which must be worse even than having molesworth 2 for a bro. You can imagine wot goes on in the fotherington-tomas home.

ARABELLA FOTHERINGTON-TOMAS (*who is knitting* 5000 *yards of woollen reins*): i am so glad our cotage is called swete lavender.

FOTHERINGTON-TOMAS (*looking up from his story about wee tim in chatterbox*): so am i. There are brownies living in the dust-bin. i saw one this morning.

ARABELLA: Hurrah that makes me feel hapy.

F-T.: Sing me your skool song arabela.

ARABELLA (*at once*):

> Ho for bat Ho for ball
> Ho for hockey and lax and all
> miss dennis is strict,
> miss hamilton fair
> But miss peabody (gym) is both strict and
> tall.

(*There is a mighty racket outside. molesworth hammers on the door*)

Open in the name of beelzebub.

But so grate is the noise of the skool song that noone come so wot is there left for me to do? i climb into the fairy coach whip up the mice into a gallop and zoom away.

BULIES

Every skool hav a resident buly who is fat and roll about the place clouting everybode. This is nesessessery so that we can all hav a sermon from time to time chiz e.g. *if you are strong remember the little felow. Give him a helping hand*

Every skool hav a resident buly who is fat

do not bash him up. Perhaps he hav been anoying perhaps he have said you have a face like a squashed tomato. Wot of it? Perhaps the little felow is right. You have got a face like a sqashed tomato. Ect.

well you kno how they go on.

There are 2 kinds of buly. There are fat bulies who can run fast and fat bulies who can't run for tooffe. There is nothing to be done about fat bulies who can run xcept to be polite to them e.g. *good morning grabber you bilge rat pax pax pax pax. i didn't mean it really i didn't ow ow paxpaxpax.*

On the whole this is hardly satisfactory.

Bulies who can't run are beter. You can watch them swanking up the coridor then zoom past chanting Look at the clot-faced wet. Buly turn red as a beetroot and stump after you like a giant but too late you have melted into the distance hem-hem. 3 days later buly come up to you when you are sitting at your desk. He sa : Look here molesworth you called me a clot-faced wet wot do you mean by it? Then you shake your head. Me? No dash it honestly word of honour (fingers crossed) I would not dream of using such uncouth words. Somebody else must hav thort you were a clot-faced wet as well.

WAM.

But the nimble molesworth have skipped litely away the buly is left cursing. Bulies are pathetic objects whom i diskard. There is only this. Just let a junior tick call me a clot-faced wet in 2 years time and you'll see what i'll do.

SNEKES

Everyone kno wot snekes are they are unspekable but they abound in every skool e.g. i am just cutting up my bungy under cover of the blotch in preparation for all-out barrage when sneke sa

LOOK AT WOT MOLESWORTH IS DOING BEHIND HIS BLOTCH, SIR.

The master look up dreamily from his novel of love and passion. He sees nothing his eyes are glazed he is still with the hero and GURL in the desert. Besides he ma not want to think wot i am doing behind the blotch it might be more than his delikate nerves can take.

HE IS CUTTING UP HIS INDIARUBER SIR IN CONTRAVENTION OF SKOOL RULE 66 (c) para 3.

The master come to earth.

'I supose that is true, molesworth,' he sa. He stretches languidly for the punishment book. 'The usual, molesworth. Put it away and get on.'

This is the signal for the whole klass to sizzle like a steam engine saing 'Sneke sneke sneke.' Sneke looks highly delighted with himself and put out his tongue. He will be the hon sec of a tenis club when he grow up and serve him right no fate is too bad. Master give long sigh and take up his novel agane. The beaitful lydia parkington is better than j. caesar so i do not blame him.

Gabbitas creeps round the wood one way

5

HOW TO BE TOPP
IN ENGLISH

i have said there only one peom in the english language e.g.
The Brook which chater chater as it flo my dear it is
obviously a girlie just like fotherington-tomas. However
there are other peoms which creep in from time to time
there is one which go

> *Har fleag har fleag har fleag onward*
> *Into the er rode the 600.*

There are as well lars porsena of clusium elegy in country
churchyard loss of the royal george and chevy chase.
Anything to do with dafodils is also grate favourite of
english masters but then nothing is beyond them they
will even set burns (rabbie) who is uterly weedy.

It is farely easy to be topp in english and sometimes you
may find yourself even getting interested. If that happens
of course you can always draw junctions and railway lines
on your desk viz

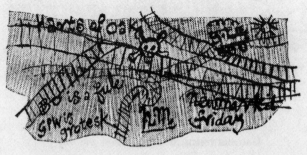

EXPRESSION

Sometimes english masters make you *read* peoms chiz chiz chiz. You have to sa the weedy words and speke them beaitfully as if you knew what they meant. Fotherington-tomas thinks this is absolutely super and when he sa he wander lonely as a cloud you think he will flote out of the window. Some cads roters and swots love to read they beg for the chance and put their hands up saing sir sir sir please sir as if they are in agony. English masters who are always perverse then sa molesworth go on CHIZ.

SIR THE BURIAL SIR OF SIR JOHN MOORE SIR AT CORUNNA SIR

(*A titter from 2B they are wet and i will tuough them up after.*)

Notadrumwasheardnotafuneralnote
shut up peason larffing
As his corse
As his corse
what is a corse sir? gosh is it
to the rampart we carried
(*whisper you did not kno your voice was so lovely*)
Not a soldier discharged his farewell shot.
PING!
Shut up peason i know sir he's blowing peas at me
Oer the grave where our hero we buried.

(*A pause a grave bow i retire and Egad! peason hav placed a dainty pin upon mine seat.* Fie!)

Occasionally you can work a wizard wheeze that the english master reads. This is not so difficult becos all masters like to show how it should be done. They look very grave turn the pages and announce

THE RETURN OF THE CHIFF-CHAFF

The class palpitate with excitement at the prospect of so exciting a story. Master slowly and sadly cast his eye to the ceiling and then down to the book while pupils prepare huge dumps of ammunition, train guns and ease atomic catapults.

MAGISTER: (*in a deep sad voice*) The chiff-chaff, the comon warbler of his moorland district, was now abundant, more so than anywhere else in England. (*BONK*) two or three were flitting about (*eeeauowoooo – WAM*) within a few feet of my head give me that peashooter molesworth and a dozen at least were singing within hearing (*ur-ur-ur-ur-ur-ur*) chiff-chaffing near and if this noise continues i shall stop reading and give you some parsing far, their notes sounding strangely loud at that still, sequestered spot. (*CRASH BONK WAM WHIZZ*)

Listening to that insistent sound I was reminded of Warde Fowler's words please sir, molesworth is strangling me stand on your chair molesworth CRASH words about the sweet season which brings new life and hope to men there is no need to cry fotherington-tomas and now a BONK and BANG is CRASH on it by that same bird's ur-ur-ur-ur-ur-ur eeeauowooo –

(*MAGISTER continues nothing can stop him while the ELEVES disport themselves merrily each small one to his own inclinations. It is thus indeed that n. molesworth acquired that grate love for english literature which was such a comfort to him in later years hem-hem.*)

What it all amounts to is that english is chiefly a matter of marksmanship. You can always come topp if you lay the rest of the class out but as auden sa so witily no cracked shot can hit every time. Ho fie lo egad and away for it is the BELL and it tolleth for me cheers cheers cheers.

THE MOLESWORTH DAY-DREAM
SERVICE 2

THE SPACE-SHIP TAKES OFF

EEEeeeeeaouh space ship away inside all is quiet as Captain molesworth the interplanetary clot eases the controls towards uranus. An hour later they touch down.

'Late as usual,' grumble molesworth 2.

LOOK OUT!

A poisoned projectile from mars embedd itself in the uranium. As they bend to pick it up 150 treen pirate rockets pancake down beside them.

'Now i hav you capt. molesworth,' grit the PUKON, the MASTER MIND. 'Hav you anything to declare?'

'2 pairs of nylons, some old bungy and the skool dog.'

'Arrest him!'

The treens step forward and bind him.

'WOW, O PUKON.' they sa.

'Put him in the reactor, o clot-faced doodlebugs.'

'The reactor is full, O PUKON. You always put the earth men there and they always escape it is very depressing. It is the same with the furnaces and the steel doors. Always get out at the last moment.'

'Try the moon-crater full of monsters.'

'Full too, O PUKON.'

'Dash it,' snarl the PUKON but as he speak Capt. molesworth's fist smash into his jaw . . . . . .

Go on, molesworth.

Er what, sir?

We hav been reading the water babies molesworth in turn round the class is it possible that you hav not been following?

yes sir of course sir.

then pray continue but i see you canot. It would appere boy that mrs doasyouwouldbedoneby does not amuse you that the

adventures of tom the sweep are shall we sa somewhat insippid
that chas. kingsly's matchless prose is perhaps a trifle demode
It would appere also boy that you have beter thorts, a suficient
knoledge a master grasp . . . . . .

ect. ect. ect. ect. ect. ect. Class think this all highly
amusing chiz chiz and larff like anything and thus the
gosamer SPELL is broken. Pon my soul dear darling
arabela but LIFE is tuough.

6

WIZZ FOR GAMES

Skool acording to headmaster's pi-jaw is like LIFE chiz if that is the case wot is the use of going on? There must be give and take, fair weather and foul, triumph and disaster but he do not give the exact proportions. Anyway finaly he come to it. There must be WORK – yes but WORK and PLA. You have guessed wot is coming next it is inevitable. ALL WORK AND NO PLA MAKES JACK A DULL BOY. i don't kno about Jack but in my case it is certainly not *that* which hav made me dull. It is all pla and no work but let it pass.

Headmasters hav to hav some sort of excuse for games so that they can drive all boys and masters out into the foul and filthy air while they stir the coals into a blaze and setle down with one of the gangster books they have confiskated. In the last 5 minits they appear on the touchline and shout GET INTO HIM MOLESWORTH GET INTO HIM it is all very well i am cold and covered with mud the only thing i want to get into is a bath ha-ha.

And talking of baths they are all mighty ones at our skool. It take you 3 days to climb up the side and when you get to the topp it might be everest giddy heights and a sheer drop into icy water. There are 3 elks which turns each of the huge brass taps but the cold elks work harder than the HOT chiz. Zoom down the side with a mighty slide and not so much as a st. bernard dog with a keg of the STUFF to revive you but wot hav all this to do with games eh. Games are not bad and they foster our natural development (official).

Batsmanship

1. The stance

2. Left leg towards the ball

3. Eye on the ball

4. Swing of the bat

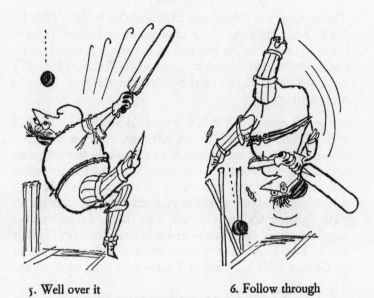

5. Well over it

6. Follow through

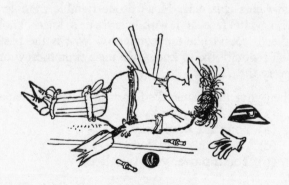

7. The Final Phase

CRIKET

There is only one thing in criket and that is the STRATE
BAT. Keep yore bat strate boy and all will be all right in
life as in criket. So headmasters sa, but when my bat is strate
i still get bowled is that an omen chiz. Aktually i usually
prefer to hav a slosh: i get bowled just the same but it is
more satisfactory.

For the reason that it is extremely dificult to hit the ball
with a STRATE BAT or not criket matches are a bit of a
strane. When you are a new bug or a junior in the 3rd game
it is all right becos then you can sit around the boundary
and keep the score in a notebook. When you get tired with
that which is about 3 minits you can begin to tuough up
your frendes and neighbours who look so sweet and
angelic in their clean white criket shirts hem-hem. This is
super. You look up long enuff to sa Good shot, grabber
or Couldn't hit a squashed tomato and then back to the
fray.

But it is a funy thing when you grow biger you always
get into a criket team you canot avoid it chiz. Tremble
tremble you arive and see the pitch which is 2388 miles
approx from the pavilion. Captain win toss and choose to
bat chiz chiz chiz chiz. Moan drone tremble tremble you
sit with white face and with everybode's knees knoking
together it sound like a coconut shy. Wot is the pleasure
of it eh i would like to kno. Give me a thumbscrew or slo
fire every time.

When your turn come the folowing things can hapen

    (A) You loose your bat.

    (B) You fante dead away.

    (C) Your trousis fall down.

    (D) You trip over your shoe laces.

Captain then come up to you and sa BLOCK EVERY-
THING molesworth and do not slosh we need 6 to win.

SOOLILOQUY

Let us pause a while and consider. Ah-me. As i stand here at mid-of how petty it all seme. These flaneled fules, the umpires, the headmaster who bask in his deck chair. All those latin books inside, the shavings in the carpentry shop the japes and wheezes – so much toil so much efort. And it may all be ended in a moment.

When he sa this all the things above hapen all at once.
They revive you with a buket of water and drive you out to
the wicket. This is not as you guessed 2398 miles away it
is 6000 now and they hav men with gats covering all the
exits so you canot run away.

AT THE WICKET

Of course it is the fast blower you hav to face he is wating
there at the other end of the pitch looking very ferce.
Umpire is v. kind he can aford to be he hav not got to bat.
He sa

We are very pleesed to see you do make yourself at
home. Of course you would like guard what guard would
you like us to give you?

Squeak.

Come agane?

Squeak squeak.

i will give you centre hold your bat up strate to you a
trifle now away agane. That is centre. Your position is 120
miles NNE of beachy head you may come in and land.
There are 5 balls to come. At the 5th pip it will be 4. 2
precisely. Able Baker Out.

PLAY !

Fast blower retreat with the ball mutering and cursing.
He stamp on the grass with his grate hary feet he beat his
chest and give grate cry. Then with a trumpet of rage he
charge towards you. Quake quake ground tremble birdseed
fly in all directions if only you can run away but it is not
done. Grit teeth close eyes. Ball hit your pads and everyone
go mad.

OWSATSIR OW WASIT EHOUT!

Umpire look for a long time he is bent double at last he
lift one finger.

He is a difrent man now from the kindly old gentleman
who made you feel at home. His voice is harsh.

Distance back to pavilion is now 120000 miles

Out. No arguments. Get cracking. Take that xpresion off your face. On course at 20000 feet return to base. Out.

Distance back to pavilion is now 120000 miles and all the juniors sa yar boo sucks couldn't hit a squashed tomato. It is no use saing you were not out by a mile team give you the treatment behind the pav just the same. There is only one consolation you can give it up when you grow up. Then you rustle the paper and sa Wot a shocking show by m.c.c. most deplorable a lot of rabits ect. ect. Well, you kno how they go on. Enuff.

FOOPBALL

Foopball is a tuough game but it is a pity you canot win by hacking everbode. You hav to be nippy. You hav also to be agile cuning alert skeming courageous and imbecile. But there are a few of us who are only imbeciles cheers cheers cheers and just do wot we can to pla our humble part in that well-oiled foopballing machine which is the st custards eleven i.e. thro mud cakes at fotherington-tomas, encourage skool dog to trip referee and diskuss influence of t. s. eliot on 20th century drama with a few progresive-thinking players of like interests. Another thing we do to cheet the long hours of boredom of the foopball field on a winters afternoon is to diskuss composition of all-time world eleven

WORLD XI
Goliath.

Romulus.   Remus.

Skool dog.   self.   Richard 1.

Julius Caesar. Cain. Jack the Ripper. Livy. Esau.

●

Ref. Solomon.

i think a few of those would hold their own in any company and there mite even be a revolution in foopball methods.

MATCHES

st custards was agog with excitement on the day of the match with their grate rivals, porridge court. And then came the blo which spread consternation through the skool making faces in maths classes glumer even than ushual. Hary mugwort, the briliant centre forward, had been put into deten by sigismund the mad maths master for saing BANG whenever a perpendicular was droped. He must miss the match and who would take his place? nigel molesworth was quietly tuoughing up the junior ticks when the footer captain tapped him on the shoulder. 'You are in the team, molesworth,' he sa. 'Gratters.'

'OO gosh wot me. Where will i pla eh?'

'Centre forward.'

molesworth then fanted and was revived by the larffter of the junior ticks.

'oo ha-ha-ha-ha look at baby molesworth who couldn't kick a flea ect. He thinks he is going to be the hero of the match but we kno beter. Much beter. We kno the match is as good as lost Hahahaha.'

*   *   *

Hurra! a mighty cheer broke as porridge court scored their eighth gole. With only 5 minits to go the match looked safe for this unsemely colection of huge louts and bulies.

'Come on st custards,' sa the footer captain cheerfuly. 'Only 8 goles down. We can do it. Pla up and pla the game.'

'8 goles?' sa molesworth. 'Gosh.'

So far he had not touched the ball except to tap it off from the centre. He had been the weak link in the chain. Now he determined to pla his natural game. Instead of a tap he kicked off with a tremendous boot at the gole. The ball stuned the fuleback and went into the gole. One to st custard's. Porridge court kicked off only for molesworth to gane posession and do it agane. He scored from all quarters of the field – 2, 3, 4, 5, 6, 7, 8 and, in the last seconds, a mighty crash from a gole kick drove the ball into the porridge court net to win the match. Hurra! The exultant spektators dashed across the field to chair their hero into the pav. . . . . .

Poor saps, i supose you believed all that. You lapped it up, eh, like all those skoolboy stories. But life is not like that. It is not like wot dickens and all those write either.

A REEL MATCH

I am sorry to sa it but in reel life foopball matches are a bit diferent. First the porridge court team arive they all look like giants tuough tuough but with blue knees. They hav a keen master with them who sa 'Warm up knees bend got your coshes. Each of you get into your man and maim him. Here are your gloves golekeeper the lead is inside.'

He then go off to the touchline to cheer and exhort. The rest of st custard's then arive saing yar boo sucks while masters lash them with knouts. They are then herded at pistol point and made to sing st custard's cheer

> *Boom-walla boom walla*
> *Geese walla geese walla*
> *st custard's hooray!*

At this moment gold-plated rolls royce arive with visiting headmaster. Headmasters greet each other.

Well how are you hoggwart eh wot eh.[1] We hav not a bad team won all our last six matches quite promising.[2] Of course we are up to 99 boys can't get another bed in the place.[3] And of course royalty is a great responsibility for all.[4] But we are building up quite a little shall we sa kno-how [5] in that direction ha-ha.

REEL THORTS OF ST CUSTARD'S HEADMASTER

1. Older and fatter bad colour.
2. Buys his players wot was the transfer fee.
3. Curses curses.
4. Wait till they ask for the porn ticket on the crown jewels.
5. Kno-how? treble fees and toothpaste extra.

Peep! the shrill whistle go (keats) the match begin. Headmasters charge up and down the touchline belowing at the tops of their voices.

COME ON PORRIDGE COURT LETS HAV A GOLE. PILE INTO YOUR MEN. MARK THEM. CROSBY-KERSHAW-PARKINSON (Hon. The A.P.R.)

Thring creeps round the other way

MARK YOUR MAN. FOUL! SEND HIM OFF! WILL MILORD KINDLY GET HIS FAT HEAD TO THE BALL? IF YOUR HIGHNESS WILL PERMIT ME AFFAIRS OF STATE ARE NOT MORE IMPORTANT THAN CRASHING THE LEATHER INTO THE RETICULE. NO SWEET PRINCE NOT YOUR OWN RETICULE YOU SEE WOT YOU HAV DONE. ON AGANE PORRIDGE COURT ECT.

It is a funy thing tho your side always gets beaten which-ever skool you are at. That is like life i supose. fotherington-tomas skips about when he is golie 'Hullo trees Hullo birds.' ect. He luv only bountiful nature and perhaps he is right.

SHOOTING

This sounds more fun than it aktualy is. They lend you a gun it is true but you are not alowed to shoot anything you realy want to chiz i.e. masters, the matron, robins, etc. chiz. You could hav wizard fun if you pretend they were red indians chiz but you hav to aim at a weedy target. You mite get a bird of fotherington-tomas by mistake like this but there is not much chance. Besides, they always tell you not to point a gun. If you do not point it wot use *is* a gun i would like to kno?

SWIMING

Agane the iron hand of authority prevent us from geting the best out of swiming which would otherwise be full of belyflopers, duckings atomic splashes and the shouts and cries of those who perish. Insted we are suspended like a spider chiz on the end of a pole and told to strike out. Most boys in this position do not strike out but suck in which do not help. if i had my way i would be a frogman and look super in a ruber suit and webbed feet but pop sa it is rather xpensive. Anyway peason tell me i look like a frogman without suit or feet chiz chiz so i stooge off to punkture fotherington-tomas ickle pritty water wings.

CONKERS

Conkers is an old-fashioned game which hav been played by generations of british boys. You kno what hapens you pick up a huge horse chestnut which look absolutely super like a derby winner and put some string through it. Then you chalenge grabber or gilibrand who hav a conkerer of 20. You say weedy things like

> Obbly obbly onker
> My first conker
> Hay ho hay nonny no ect.

Honour your oponent and turn round on the points of your toes. After that you whirl your conker round and hurl it at the dangling target hem-hem. Successful conkers are always shriveled and weedy. Wot hapens is that your conker either shaters into a milion pieces or flies through the nearest window crash crash tinkle tinkle. ('i shall make you pay from your poket-money, molesworth, not becos i *need* the money but becos you must face the conse-quences of your actions.')

What is needed in conkers is a new scientific approach. We are too conservative. As new elizabethans we must adventure with science i.e. select a new conker bombard it with uranium 238 (element 92) folow it with a beam of nitrogen atoms fired from a 60 inch cyclotron. If it stands this all the neutrons will hav gummed together in a nucleus. If it do not, turn the cyclotron on molesworth 2 or fotherington-tomas and see wot it do to them. If they disintegrate in less than 2.3 minits the thanks of mankind should be yours but you may be ahead of your time chiz.

SNAKES AND LADERS

If you hav a quiet half hour with one of your dear companions like peason or gillibrand what is nicer than a game of snakes and laders? Aktualy quite a number of things are nicer like a film of marylyn monroe a quiet cig or a plateful of roste turkey but you do not get these things at skool chiz so it have to be snakes and laders.

How to Play. Face oponent and lay all gats and coshes on the hall table. Setle the stakes at 5 bob a corner. Inspect dice. Turn round and tuough up junior ticks for looking. Start cheerfuly go up laders cheers cheers go down snakes. Dice fly and are lost in w.p.b. Stare at snakes and observe resemblance to certain of your contemporaries hem-hem. Go down snake and start agane. Now not so cheerful. Oponent come down. More cheerful. This go on until you are 997 years old and dying of old age. You could take up chess instead but you may find the game too fast.

THE GYMNASIUM

Wot makes a boy healthy and splendid with giant and ripling muscles? Wot makes his torso remarkable eh? The answer is not the red ink skull and crossbones on his chest or the tatoo marks i luv maysie on his biceps. The effect is obtained by his WORK in the GYM.

As in other departments of skool life SUKSESS do not always come easily. In fact the grate gymnasiums of Britain are littered with boys who hav broken their legs, brused their branes (if any) grazed their shins and sufered horibly. You can always tell where the gym is becos all the vultures hover over it and each time the springboard go PLUNK they strane their ears and their mouths water. THAT boy was safely over the horse (and the gym sergeant too) but sooner or later one will make a slip. He will fall out of the line tallest on the right shortest on the left and be deserted to his fate.

The Horse

Every gymnasium hav a horse for the tiny tots to jump over. At one end is a springboard and there is also a scrufy old thing lying on the floor at the other. This is not the gym sergeant who hav had too much BEER it is the MAT and if you landed on the gym sergeant instead you would soon kno the diference and learn some interesting WORDS.

The BOY BEATIFUL who is determined to be good at gym rev. up like mad zoom away bounce on the springbord and sale litely over the horse. Sometimes however he make a bish. When that hapen he bounce on the springbord rise verticaly in the air and strike his head on the roof. When you come to think of it there is no reason why this should not hapen more often than it do.

The Bar

No not that kind of bar clot altho anebode would need a stiff tot before he can do 3 circles with no hands. Aktualy the whole thing is simply pappy. You sit erect on the bar bak holow arms stiff eyes fixed in glassy stare and whole face contorted with fear. After about 3 hours trying to pluck up courage this position becomes a bit uncomfortable. Besides the mob ten miles below get a bit restless. They sa Yar Boo Sucks and cowardy cowardy custard and other weedy things. You then decide to go. Then you change your mind the whole affair is too ghastly.

Position 2. Thro the arms upwards and bakwards swing with the bar in the crook of your knobbly knees. Round round round out and down. All you need really is Confidence. You must not believe for a moment that it is posible that you can go round round round down and OUT. Just give a good swing to start with and all will be well. If it isn't you won't kno anything about it aneway.

Position 3. The final position. Rigid, unconscious, chin in, hands stretched to sides, nose and toes in air. (Too much movement may damage the stretcher.)

The Rings

The rings are the most dangerous of all and only a really tuough and brave BOY BEATIFUL can show off with them. There are two rings and they hang down on two ropes at least they do unless some skoolboy who luv pranks hav severed them with his jackknife. Wot you hav to do is to swing on the rings in some very funy positions. You can be chest out or chest in or arms xtended. But there is only one rule i can give e.g. HOLD ON. If you let go you fly out of the window. And then where will you be poor thing? In the rubish bin along with the skool brekfast poo gosh which is most unsavoury.

Another exercise with the rings is to swing on them by yore feet upside down. This is super. At least it would be if fotherington-tomas do not come along.

'Look at me fotherington-tomas,' you sa as you zoom by. 'Look at me no hands.'

'i am looking,' he sa. 'Wot are you doing?'

'Boddy swinging ARMS XTENDED, feet in the rings bakwards and forwards bending with deep rhymical breething.'

'So that is the noise i hear?'

'In and O-U-T. In and O-U-T.'

(*fotherington-tomas scratch his head.*)

'But molesworth wot is the *point* of it?' he sa. 'Wot hav you ganed when it is all over? Do it make you beter than other boys? Wot does it *prove* in the long run? ect. ect.' . . . . . .

These are very dificult questions to answer when swinging by the feet upside down. As you ponder you strike head sharply on the ground.

'You see?' sa fotherington-tomas and stroll away. He is a gurly.

7

HOW TO BE TOPP
IN FRENCH

Whenever anyone mention fr. all the eleves sa oo gosh ugh french weedy ect but it is no use saing what's the use of it as you do with latin. The masters sa fr. is a living langwage and swank about they think they hav got the beter of us chiz. It is not much use repling O.K. bruther SO WHAT when fr. masters sa fr. is living it is beter to be keen cheerful and enthusiastick

e.g. The Francais, sir, are certainly vital and ebullient.
or

The Francais realy understand the art of LIFE don't you agree, monsieur?

Monsieur may not be fuled by this but it may lead to something. In fact it may lead to him teling you about his last holiday in Dieppe tho i would hav thought the less said about what he did *there* the beter. This may tempt a tiny eleve to get caried away and GO TOO FAR e.g. were there any mademoiselles hem-hem there, monsieur?

No master like his name coupled with a GURL at least not by a garcon they are not pray to mortal passions. Next moment the whole class is back with Armand and M. Dubois and the other weeds in the fr. book. (leson 3 etre to be ect.)

ALL ABOUT ARMAND

Everyone kno that Armand is a wet becos he wear that striped shirt and sissy straw hat. In Lesson 6A Armand has just entered into the salle a manger from the jardin. He enter it not to pinch something to eat but to give Mama the jolies fleurs which he hav picked. Papa is pleased. Papa is not woried as he joly well ort to be at this base conduct. Papa is highly delited.

'Thou art a good boy, Armand,' he sa, 'this afternoon i will take thee to the zoo.'

Ahha you think Papa is not so dumb as he look he will thro Armand to the lions.

'Are there any animals in the zoo?' ask Armand.

'Oh but yes,' sa Papa without loosing his temper at this feeble question.

'Houpla houpla i am so hapy.'

Perhaps the lions are not bad enough perhaps it will hav to be the loups. The loups could indubitably do a good job on Armand. Is it with these thoughts that Papa go hand in hand with his little son? They pay ten sous. They pass through the turnstile. They enter into the zoological garden. They look around themselves.

'How big the elephants are,' observe Armand at length.

'Yes and also the giraffes.'

'The monkeys are amusings.'

'O yes en effet and there is a fox.'

'Foxes are naughties.'

You wonder if it was noel coward who wrote the dialog it is so nervously brilliant my dear how long can it be before Papa do Armand. But it is not to be. They pass the loups and the lions but o hapen chiz xcept that Papa observe that the sky is blue altho it is sometimes grey. They go out of the turnstile and return home.

'Next week we will go a la campagne,' sa Papa.

Now you can see what hav been going on. The zoo and the bord de la mer are too crowded. Get Armand by himself in a meadow and it is money for jam unless aunt beatrice goes along. Then Papa can do them both or they can watch the bees flit from flower to flower. It is up to him.

'How big the elephants are,' observe Armand

A STRATAGEM HEM-HEM

Altho fr. masters canot keep order they stick grimly to their task nothing seme to discourage them. It is a good wheeze then if you have a real Fr. boy in the class. Then you sa innocently

What is it like in France, sir?

France is quite exquisit molesworth the fine old wines of Burgundy the splendid food the gay wines of Champagne the cafes the railway stations the mice which love cheese and the trees which are pretty.

Gosh sir really sir then it is just like the piktures in the fr. book?

France molesworth do not hav beetles drawn all over it. Get on with your ex. boy.

This is the time when you stick your compass into the real Fr. boy who jaber like a bren gun

maymsieuestcequejaituailaspaparat ect. for 5 minits. Then there is silence you could here a piece of buble gum drop and fr master larff uneasily

Come again le crapaud he sa come again.

well you kno what it is once a fr. boy start you canot stop them becos they hav so much on their mind.

i only venture to remark he sa that recevoir is a verb which is the invention of the english especially in the imperfect subjunc which the grate poet beaujolais rarely if ever used in his verses assur yourself of my distinguished sentiments ect.

'Cor!'

if i may have the pleasur of continuing i would sa *deuxfrancsilserontbonmieuxmeileur* ect.

'EH?'

etparcequequand and so it go on the trouble is that once a fr. boy start you canot stop him in fact you feel sory for the fr. master in a sort of way chiz. But fr. masters kno how to cope they unroll a huge pikture of a farmyard and point out a turkey.

'What is the fr. for *that*, molesworth he sa.

well i mean to sa the only one i kno on that picture is the little baby who is uterly wet he is stroking a sheep. No wonder the sheep look disgusted. Anyway no boy could admit that so my lips are sealed. Dinde dolt or dindon sa the fr. master back on the home ground after loosing away.

In the midst of all these sordid transactions molesworth the magican switches off. His mouth open his plate fall out doodlebugs fall from his hair he rev the engines up and take off into the ether for another daydream.

PAS DEVANT L'ENFANT

GUIDE TO FRENCH BY GROWN UPS

	WITH MOLES-WORTH THORTS
av-ez voo ach-et-ay le gin?	have you bought the gin to replace that which we inadvertently finished last night? (*m. thinks: i prefer the other brand reelly*)
VOTRE PERE est absolument la derriere.	Your father is the absolute rock bottom. (*m. thinks: the old music hall jokes how true how true*)
av-ez vu lu ce cas dans le newsoftheworld	hav you read that shocking case in the news of the world? (*Thinks: stale old bird.*)
voo-voo soo-ven-ez de la scan-dale de mrs higginbotham?	You remember the scandal about mrs higginbothom. (*m. thinks: only too well only too well. Look at her husband you have to make allowances.*)
ce sacre cochon d'un menager de la banque.	That hem-hem (swearing conduct mark) of a bank manager. (*m. thinks: i don't kno why all this fuss about bank managers. They are only doing their job. thriftlessness brings pane in its wake.*)
Quand attend-ell le bebe?	When is she expecting the baby? (*m. thinks: in about 3 weeks.*)

Gabbitas and Thring trap a young
man and lead him off to be a master

8

EXTRA TEW

No one but skoolboys kno what extra tew is extra lesons
for bakward boys which keep aged masters out of the dog's
home becos they get paid for it and so they should. Most
extra tew is about subjects you don't kno e.g. lat. fr. algy.
geom. hist. geog. bot. div. arith. But sometimes there is
extra tew in littleknown subjects which are likely to be of
advantage in that snug nitch in the foreign office hem-hem
which is your pater and maters ambition for their hansome
nigel ho ho look at me. This kind of extra tew is very
special and include german, scandinavian literature, deport-
ment, debrett's peerage, ruffs guide to the turf *inter alia* as
we sa at brekfast. I hav never really had extra tew but i
hav my spies and this is what goes on.

SPANISH

Nobody kno much about Spanish except the Spaniards
whose beards are all singed and they are very proud and
like sherry just as some others about this place whose names
i will not mention. All this is the reason why you hav to lisp
when you speke spanish which make it all very dificult.

*there: A hathienda. Enter don jereth de la frontera moleth-
worth.*
A THERVANT: who ith it?
DON JERETH: it ith only me ith ithabel ethpecting me?
A THERVANT: Yeth.
DON J.: O thuper!
  (*he folowth the thervant*)

ithabel! my thoul-mate! ith there any therry in the house?

ITHABEL: yeth. pour out 2 slugth and i will thip with thee.

DON J.: thplendid! good thow! Cheerth! Over the fallth. (*he drinkth*) What ith that thound?

ITHABEL: Thantoth it is my bro Thantoth thipping his therry. He ith thupping with uth.

DON J.: (*thwearing*) Curseth!

That is the sort of thing which hapens with spanish and anyone who decide to kno about it is a fule.

RUSIAN

How many days till the end of term, o molesvitch 2? Some sa 20, others 90, little bro, is the fruit upon the aple tree in the orchard? Only the blosom so you will hav to wait a month or two before you can pinch them o measly weed it is 2006 miles to Moscow. Who cares sa fotherington tomas from a corner of the room where he hav been trussed up who cares a row of butons. i love only robins. Unless you love robins father christmas will not bring you any presents. A volley of shots ring out. WAM! 900 robins bite the dust. That only leaves father christmas, i sa, how flat life is . . . . . .

The swots tell me that rusian used to be like that chiz but it is all diferent now everybode is joly and at xmas time just when you are deciding whether to ask for a motor bike or a platinum watch an xciting envelop is pushed through the leter box.

'How thrilling,' sa molesworth 2 the youngest of the kiddies. 'What can it be?'

'It *feels* thrilling!' i sa coyly just like the weeds in chaterbox. 'It may be a tiny toy from aunt drusila our very xciting aunt from north wales.'

'Sometimes i think she is *too* xciting, dear nigel,' sa molesworth 2 pensively. How joly our xmas hols will be. Let us take the envelop to dear Mama and Dada.

So saing he imprint 3 huge finger prints from his hary hand and skip awa to the kitchen folowed by his larffing elder bro. Dada is washing up in the sink Mama is peeling potatoes Liza dear fatheful liza the maid is smoking a cig over a cup of tea.

'Mama mama,' the 2 sturdy little felows cry, 'Open our leter. Please open it.'

Mama do as she is bid having put the potato knife out of temptation's way. This is what she read:

И ам гивинг а литтл парти
I am giving a little party
ат ди Кремлин. ви вилл хав фун.
at the Kremlin. We will hav fun.
Маленков
Malenkov

'How nice of Mr Malenkov!' cry Mama. 'Of course you can go!'

'And may i wear my velveteen breeches and lace colar, mama?'

'Wow!' lisp wee molesworth 2 turning a somersault and the whole family join in the harty larff when he end in the dog bowl. Even towser bark but that was becos molesworth 2 had pinched his bone.

At last the day come and the 2 little chaps drive off to the Kremlin in their best suits. You can imagine what they look like. Mr Malenkov stand beaming on the steps and waiting behind him are lots of kind uncles. You can imagine the fun they all had with the tommy guns before the sir roger de coverley start: the air is thick with cordite.

Molesvitch

'Children children,' sa mr malenkov. 'Not too rough before the musical chairs.'

And so with flushed hapy faces the children join in the fun until it is time to go home.

'Come along any time,' said Mr Malenkov, as he sa goodbye, 'and I will take you both for a ride.'

That is about all there is to rusian but i supose it is more than enuff. Personaly i cant stand parties which hav dancing and eton colars and GURLS ugh. There seems to be some point in a party like that but it is too much to hope we can hav one at our home chiz. rat-tat i have 3 leters for ermintrude if she will come outside and get them BAM BIFF WALLOP folowed by SILENCE. i wouldn't mind paing a forfeit for that.

ADVANCED MATHS

All maths is friteful and means O but if you are a grate brane you hear a tremendous xplosion at about the fifth lesson in trig. This mean that you are through the sound barier and maths hav become what every keen maths master tell you it can be i.e. a LANGWAGE. in my view this is just another of those whopers which masters tell i mean can you imagine peason and me at brake:

MOLESWORTH: (*taking a hack at the pill*) $x^2 \times y^6 = a$
PEASON: $z^8 - x^3 = b$
MOLESWORTH: (*missing completely*) O, y^{99}!

As you will see it simply will not do i am prepared to believe that a strate line if infinitely protracted go on for ever tho i do not see how even that weed pythagoras can tell. But if maths is a langwage i hav only one coment. It is

$$\sum_0^\infty \frac{b^x}{x!} = \sum_0^\infty \frac{e^{-M} \cdot M^x \cdot e^{tx}}{x!} = e^{-M} \sum_0^\infty \frac{(Me^t)^x}{x!}$$

I think that setles the mater.

MUSIC LESSONS

Kno Yore Instrument. This is the skool piano you kno the one which go WAM PLUNK BISH BASH ZUNK. It is a cranky old grid made by an old german called B.ch..ei.

co. . . .ldb..rg. As you will see it hav a pair of brass flame-throwers and a bubble for a rear gunner. The loud pedal droped off when molesworth 2 pla 'fairy bells' and hav never been seen agane. Inside there are a lot of old marbles, cig cards, toy soldiers and dead goldfish. There are a lot of wooden things which tap up and down. I think that if it hav a rebore and new piston rings it would be a snip.

The Lesson. It is easy pappy to be a grate player like molesworth 2 all you must do is recognise the notes. The fat ones you hav to hold for 4 secs. These are minims. There are a lot of weedy ones called quavers but it is difficult to get these in. There are also crotchets. I do not think anyone know this xcept mrs curwen. i can only tell you that if you get the whole lot of minims crotchets and quavers mixed up together it is like an atomic xplosion cheers cheers cheers.

The Position. You canot pla the skool piano unless you are adjusted at the right height. You can sit upon a stool and zoom to the right. This takes you up through the ladies hats, hardware, toys and a few v. unsavoury sort of places until you canot get any higher. If you go the other way you go round and round at 90 m.p.h. until you are too giddy to see. When you are like this music mistress lay you out with a hamer and all is peaceful.

The Choice. Wot will you pla? Fairy Bells ripling brook spring dances or scotish capers. You hav a long way to go before you can swing chiz like the last music mistress who was lost without trace when piano xploded.

WAM now nigel pla low C Bonk candlestick shoot into air BISH swing it baby swing it BASH PLUNK ZUNK. Give it xpresion it is a brook. La-la-la and a one BUNK two ZUNK 3 PLUNK – la-la-la the left finger. THE LEFT la-la-la – – well, eh, you see wot i mean? 3 trillion boos to tchkovsky.

9

HOW TO BE TOPP IN
ALL SUBJEKTS

The Molesworth Self-Educator

Directions. Take pencil in the right hand, revolve three times with eyes shut and DAB. You are bound to be right sooner or later.

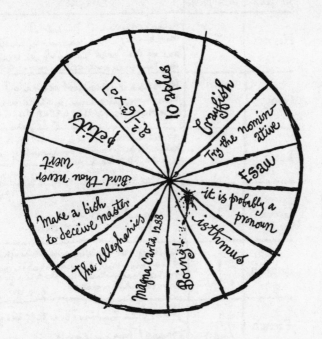

The Molesworth Bogus Report

ST. CUSTARDS.

NAME **N. Molesworth**

EXAM ORDER **1**   TERM ORDER **1**

FINAL ORDER **1**

SUBJECT	POSITION	REMARKS
History	I	Extraordinary! His Life of Marlborough was uncannily brilliant one of the best things of its kind in the present century. GUG
Geog.	1	He have a spendid sense of position, give him a globe and he know exactly what do with. P. st l. g.
Latin	1	It is seldom that we get a skolar like this who knowe all his grammer backwards. If he have a fault it is to muck quickness livy cesar tovid did not write enuff for him. but would be better if he thought they wrote in Latin. B.E.AK
Greek	1	Beyond words. B. AK
English	1 (ONE)	I didn't ought too say to much in praise of his styl did I but his essays are remarkable and have been reproduced in skool mag. Col strike a flippin lite a genius. S.T.E
French	1 (UNE)	Tres, tres tres tres tres tres bien. Bravo! Formidable. MUD.

Directions: Fill in the name and post on first day of hols.
Destroy reel report when it comes along.

SUBJECT	POSITION	REMARKS
Drawing	1	A wonderful sense of colour + line. His choice of subjects is perhaps a little doubtful. F.U.G
Music	1#	Toscananinni must beware. Benjamin Britten

HEADMASTERS REPORT

There was a time when dere nigth was rather wild and chased about the place at full tilt shouting "Down with Skool!". Now thanks to St Custard's that is all changed thanks to St custard's he have almost worked a miracle – now we see him whole skolar, poet, man of action – dilletante, wine lover, dreamer, beer drinker – coiner of phrases, wit, athlete, strongman. He is the LOT. (thanks to St Custard's) I think he should now goon from strength to strength and you can imagine with what feelings I look forward to his returning next term.

J. Duddridge Plunk

(Headmaster &
sole Licensee)

Next term begins*: } Jan. .... May .... Sept. .**31.**

MATRON'S REPORT

We forgot to pack his combs. Simply couldn't face'd.
E.F.

* Fill in one week later

10

HOW TO COPE WITH GROWN UPS

Grown ups are wot is left when skool is finished. Masters are not really grown ups they are ha-ha just spoilt children who hav to hav their own way. You kno where you are with them. One is strict another wheezes through his false teeth, a third teaches geom and a fourth teaches Less than O he just wanders about.

It is not the same with Grown Ups who were always perfect when they were young. e.g.

WHEN I WAS A BOY I WOULD NOT HAV DARED TO SPEAK TO MY FATHER LIKE THAT.

Well, you kno what this means becos obviously this is what really hapned to your pater.

Scene: An old stone breakfast table about 1066 A.D. Your pater, then known as litle Cedric, is sitting down to his groats poor litle dear when the old man Horible arive breathing through his beard.

HORIBLE (rubbing his hands): Good morning, good morning, good morning. What mammoth agane?

SPOUSE: It is very nice, my dear. Shall i pour you yore BEER?

HORIBLE: Yes, yes. Goodmorning, Cedric.

CEDRIC: YAR boo and sucks.

SPOUSE: Do not speak to your father like that, Cedric, or you will go strate to your cave. Hav you finished your groats.

CEDRIC: Yes, Mama.

SPOUSE: Then get on with your egg. And stop playing with the brontosaurus at breakfast.

HORIBLE: Yes, stop playing with the bronto –

SPOUSE: Don't buly the child let him get on.

HORIBLE (*meekly*): Yes, my dear.

(*A pause while HORIBLE opens the newspaper and the brontosaurus springs across the table.*)

HORIBLE: We are losing the test match, Cedric. Gaul hav made 2900 for 2.

CEDRIC: So what?

HORIBLE: i only –

CEDRIC: You are a sily old man who couldn't lift a cucumber.

HORIBLE: i –

CEDRIC (*chanting*): Silly old daddy couldn't hurt a flea.

SPOUSE: Stop interupting and playing with the child. For heavens sake let him get on with his egg.

CEDRIC: Yar yar yar.

(*The brontosaurus springs at HORIBLE'S plate and eats his mammoth. In despair HORIBLE go to the office.*)

So you see how it was.

Maters hav a diferent approach and they are very keen on maners ect which include not throing bungie, making lakes of treacle in the porridge, flicking bread pelets at molesworth 2 grabing the sugar, slashing gravy rivers through potatoes, reading the back of your pater's *Times*, imitating a baboon, striking your next door neighbour ect ect.

In fact you are xpected to be xactly like wee tim especially when mater's grate skool friend mabel entwhistle (prothero that was) pay a visit with her tiny dorter chiz chiz chiz. On that morning all boys cats dogs parots sparos and owls are turned into the garden while house is polished and mabel entwhistle's foto is brought out of the boxroom. Boys glue their noses against windows and are finaly admited.

'Do not the house look luvly, nigel,' sa yore mater.

'But it never look like this reely it is just an empty facade.'

'O.K.,' sa yore mater. 'But let's keep it that way, see? Otherwise there's liable to be trubble. Look at yore knees.'

i do not kno why boys are always told to look at their knees it is dashed dificult. In fact the only way is to lie on yore back and pull yore knees up. Maters, however, are liable to get batey if you do this in the sitting room just before ma entwhistle arive becos they see wot is on the soles of yore shoes. Too repulsive, my dear.

Procedure. Ho to the bathroom. Out flanel and wipe geting most off. Brush front of hair and leave back. Gaze in miror at yore strange unatural beauty. Report hopefully. Back agane. Scrub nails. Leave tap runing and soap in bottom of basin. Sa look at ickle pritty to molesworth 2 who hav to put on blue corduroys cheers cheers cheers cheers. Report back and granted certificate of hygene (ist Class Honours) also gold medal antwerp exhibition 1899.

Pijaw. Mater then give pi-jaw e.g. Now you will behave nicely won't you nigel and you won't do wot you did to cicely last time.

Oh no mater rather not.

You promise?

Oh yes and i will sa nothing about her dolly either.

And you will not shout Cave Cave here they come when they ring the bell? You will not repeat wot Daddy sa at brekfast about mabel entwhistle? Nor sa rice pud ugh at lunch.

No No dearest mama perish the thort.

You had beter not, rat.

The Works. Mabel entwhistle arive in a super car a bentley or aston martin which show that mr entwhistle hav a clue or 2 which is more than pop hav. Women thro themself into each others arms like guided missiles.

Gaze in miror at yore strange unatural beauty

'Darling darling (chiz) how lovely to see you after all these years.'

Visitor then gaze about as if she hav never seen anything more beaituful in the world in space.

'How swete your house is!

(*Thinks: a dump.*)

'nigel! this must be nigel! Wot a good-looking boy.

(*Thinks: Ugh.*)

'And your younger boy how luvley.'

If anyone can call molesworth 2 luvely you kno she is telling a whoper even blue corduroy trousers do not make him into bubles not by a long chalk so it show how empty and artificial ect. hem-hem.

Enter CICELEY entwhistle.

YOUR MATER: 'Ciceley! She's already a beauty. Such hair Such eyes' ect.

(*Thinks: Gosh wot a plane child.*)

And so it go on the lunch is cold molesworth 2 drop the sprouts ciceley can't eat the steak and all larff wot screams children are to be sure. Zoom out into the garden and ciceley folow litle does she kno gay child wot is coming to her. Enuff said. The maters jaber away until teatime and at length the ghastley day is over.

Our Ancestors

nigel is so sensitive

I was awfully stupid at lessons when I was a girl

The trousers are a little long but
I think he will grow into them

Goodbye darling Give your little
motherkins a kiss!

I don't see why you should
look ashamed of me

KITCHEN-WISE

When i was a gurl yore mater sa the butler the cook and the parlourmaid did all the work. Of course all maters are dredfully old, about 96 approx, so it may hav been possible. i just do not see wot point it hav it won't get her out of the kitchen in the present century.

Maters these days train their dear little ones to domestic duties. They are just like performing seals – they clear away, make tea, polish the silver and also WASH-UP crash bang crash smash. A mater believe we are glad to help her out if only she knew. Any rate, we hav to HELP e.g.

Give me that wiper molesworth 2 its mine mum he has got the wiper with the red edges and rather unsavoury black marks give it to *me* (*wiper part in two judgment of solomon divinity ect. Howls of rage from all.*)

Aktualy you can hav a wizard time in the kitchen and molesworth 2 pinch everything including raisins flour jam washed down with the cat's milk.

While we are on the subjekt hem-hem here is my own favourite recipe which is reely very simple.

Take one cup of flour and add water at suficient pressure to spurt all over the kitchen.

Next go to the raisin tin. Eat 3 handfulls and put a few in the cup.

Add salt mint and coffee beans.

Stir vigorously and drop on the floor. Yell out of the door Mum Mum *Mum* where's the rolling pin. Eat a jam tart and roll out thin. When you are fed-up with rolling make the whole thing into a soft ball and chuck at molesworth 2.

UNCLES

Uncles are always v. embarased when they see a small boy we seme to make them nervous and i am not surprised. They ask a lot of feeble questions before they will hand over the routine halfcrown chiz.

Your uncles are outside, sir

Scene: a gilded drawing room of grate luxury. There are thick curtains and thick carpets in fact everything is thick including the head of the small boy who is lying upon the sofa eating bullseyes and watching the television.
Enter a flunky.

Your uncles are outside, sir.

Uncles! wot a bore. But they canot be a worse bore than the television. Let them be admitted.

Enter sixteen uncles with bald heads and spectacles.

Uncles (*in chorus*): How big you hav grown, nigel, since we last saw you.

Nigel: Of course i hav grown biger you didn't expect me to grow smaler did you clots. Besides, I do not think you reely care.

Uncles: You will soon be as tall as us.

Nigel: If i canot grow taler than *that* i will give up.

(*He peels a banana*).
Proceed.

UNCLES: If we all bend down we can give you a piggy back.

NIGEL: You think we boys like that don't you? You think it makes you appere joly. You will offer to pla criket with us now, I supose?

UNCLES (*eagerly*): Yes yes. If you bowl at us on the lawn we will show off by hitting the first ball for 6 and loossing it.

NIGEL: As ushual. That is a grate joke?

UNCLES: Yes, yes. To amuse you further we will vault a 5 bar gate or –

NIGEL (*shudering*): That is enuff. Hav you all got your halfcrowns eh? There is no need to sa here is something for your money box. Just put them in my hat when you go out.

UNCLES: We will (*winking roguishly*). But before that we must pat you on the head.

NIGEL: No. no. I will take the will for the deed. And make it five bob next time – the cost of living is going up.

(*Exit uncles all wishing they were young agane and rightly too.*)

GRANDMOTHERS

Grandmothers are all very strikt and they all sa the same thing as they smile swetely over their gin and orange.

It is a grandmother's privilege to spoil her grandchildren GET OFF THAT SOFA NIGEL YOU WILL BRAKE IT.

Grandmothers are very tuough when you get them in a bate so it is beter not to zoom about among the dresden china or direct space bombs at the best tea set.

You ushually get parked on grans when your mater can stand you no longer or go abroad to winter sports (such a change from the kitchen). So you get left behind it might just as well be with jack the ripper for all they care.

Aktually grans are not bad. Gran you kno our gran is a wonderful old lade hem-hem she made munitions during the war and was also a lade porter. Now she fly round the world in comets stiring up trouble so pop sa and beating black men on the head. Pop sa why bother about an atomic bomb if you can drop gran over rusia. She would soon tell them how to manage their affairs e.g. you simply *can't* be a communist, mr malenkov. That's *quite* beyond the pale.

All grans show boys the tower of london and westminster abbey and think it so amusing when molesworth 2 sa 'So what?' when told that the crown jewels are worth five trillion pounds. After that they take you to st. pauls science museum national galery madam tussauds statue of peter pan buckingham palace and wonder why their feet hurt. Mine were simply killling me, my dear. Madam tussauds is not bad as gran sa there is a man who murded 3 people. molesworth 2 sa thats nothing i hav done 5 already he is a swank and a wet.

One chiz about gran is that she hound and persekute all shopkeepers. She take you along and you hav to listen while she send for the manager. She sa i have dealt here for 30 years why can you not deliver on tuesdays ect while i try to pretend i am not there chiz also the gorgonzola is not wot it was. Personaly i think no gorgonzola is worth sending for the manager for but it must be diferent i supose when you are 723.

A GUIDE TO AUNTS

Aunts are not bad but they are inclined to be sopy and call you darling chiz chiz chiz. Also you are just like your mater or your pater whichever hapen to be the planer. Aunts ask you how you are geting on at skool and you sa o all right may you be forgiven. Then they ask you to read to them. There is only one thing to do for aunts when they ask this e.g. take out Domby and Son and give them the LOT.

Of course you know, children, what their Uncle did to the two
little Princes in the Tower

11

DING-DONG FARELY MERILY
FOR XMAS

Xmas all grown ups sa is the season for the kiddies but this do not prevent them from taking a tot or 2 from the bot and having, it may seme, a beter time than us. For children in fact Xmas is often a bit of a strane wot with pretending that everything is a surprise. Above all father xmas is a strane. You canot so much as mention that there is no father xmas when some grown-up sa Hush not in front of wee tim. So far as i am concerned if father xmas use lang-wage like that when he tripped over the bolster last time we had beter get a replacement.

CHRISTMAS EVE

Hurra for Xmas Eve wot a scurrying there was in the moles-worth household. First of all mr molesworth issued jovially with the hamer to hang the decorations – red white purple streemers holly mistletoe lights candles snow Mery Xmas All: mrs molesworth is in the kitchen with the mince pies, all rosy and shining: and judge of the excitement of the 2 boys!

In fact, it is a proper SHAMBLES.

Pop drop the hamer on the cat in the kitchen the xmas puding xplode with a huge crash and the cat spring up the curtains. Outside the sno lie deep and crisp and ect. and just as pop fall off the steplader the WATES arive.

WATES are 3 litle gurls with a torch who go as folows:

HEE HEE HEE NOEL NOEL GO ON GURT

NO-ELL NO-ELL NO YOU RING the KING of

IS-RAY-ER-ELL.

PING! PING!

TANNER FOR THE WATES, PLEASE.

This of course is money for jam but grown ups are so intoxicated with xmas they produce a shiling. Imagine a whole weeks poket money just for that when you can get it all on the wireless anyway if you want it. Or whether you want it or not.

molesworth 2 is very amusing about carols i must sa he hav a famous carol

> *While shepherds washed their socks by night*
> *All seated on the ground*
> *A bar of sunlight soap came down ect.*

He think this is so funy he roar with larffter whenever he think of it and as he spend most of the night thinking of it i do not get much slepe chiz. i sa SHUTUP molesworth 2 SHUTUP i want to go to slepe but in vain the horid zany go cakling on. It is not as if it is funy i mean a bar of sunlight soap ha-ha well it is not ha-ha-ha-ha a bar of ha-ha-ha-ha . . . . . .

Oh well.

Another thing about xmas eve is that your pater always reads the xmas carol by c. dickens. You canot stop this aktualy although he pretend to ask you whether you would like it. He sa:

Would you like me to read the xmas carol as it is xmas eve, boys?

We are listening to the space serial on the wireless, daddy.

But you canot prefer that nonsense to the classick c. dickens?

Be quiet. He is out of control and heading for jupiter.

Noel noel go on gurt you ring

But –

He's had it the treen space ships are ataking him ur-ur-ur-*whoosh*. Out of control limping in the space vacuum for evermore unless they can get the gastric fuel compressor tampons open.

I –

Why don't they try Earth on the intercom? They will never open those tampons with only a z-ray griper. They will –

Father thwarted strike both boys heavily with loaded xmas stoking and tie their hands behind their backs. He cart them senseless into the sitting room and prop both on his knees. Then he begin:

THE XMAS CAROL by C. DICKENS
(*published by grabber and grabber*)

Then he rub hands together and sa You will enjoy this boys it is all about ghosts and goodwill. It is tip-top stuff **and** there is an old man called scrooge who hates xmas and canot understand why everyone is so mery. To this you sa nothing except that scrooge is your favourite character in fiction next to tarzan of the apes. But you can sa anything chiz. Nothing in the world in space is ever going to stop those fatal words:

Marley was dead

Personaly i do not care a d. whether Marley was dead or not it is just that there is something about the xmas Carol which makes paters and grown-ups read with grate XPRESION, and this is very embarassing for all. It is all right for the first part they just roll the r's a lot but wate till they come to scrooge's nephew. When he sa Mery Christmas uncle it is like an H-bomb xplosion and so it go on until you get to Tiny Tim chiz chiz chiz he is a weed. When Tiny Tim sa God bless us every one your pater is so overcome he burst out blubbing. By this time boys hav bitten through their ropes and make good their escape so 9000000000 boos to bob cratchit.

XMAS NITE

At last the tiny felows are tucked up snug in their beds with 3 pilow slips awaiting santa claus. As the lite go off a horid doubt assale the mind e.g. suposing there *is* a santa claus. Zoom about and lay a few traps for him (see picture)

Determin to lie awake and get him but go to slepe in the end chiz and dream of space ships. While thus employed something do seem to be hapning among the earthmen.

CRASH!

Be quiet you will wake them up. Hav you got the mecano his is the one with 3 oranges if you drop that pedal car agane i shall scream where are the spangles can you not tie a knot for heavens sake ect. ect.

It would seem that the earthmen are up to something but you are far to busy with the treens who are defending

Trap for dere Santa

the space palace with germ guns. So snore on, fair child, snore on with thy inocent dreams and do not get the blud all over you.

THE DAY

Xmas day always start badly becos molesworth 2 blub he hav not got the reel rools-royce he asked for. We then hav argument that each hav more presents than the other. A Mery Xmas everybode sa scrooge in the end but we just call each other clot-faced wets so are you you you you pointing with our horny fingers it is very joly i must sa. In the end i wear molesworth 2's cowboy suit and he pla with my air gun so all is quiet.

Then comes DINNER.

This is super as there are turkey crackers nuts cream plum puding jely and everything. We wash it down with a litle ginger ale but grown ups all drink wine ugh and this make all the old lades and grans very sprightly i must sa. They sa how sweet we are they must be dotty until pater raps the table and look v. solemn. He holds up his glass and sa in a low voice

The QUEEN. Cheers cheers cheers for the queen we all drink and hurra for england.

Then pater sa in much lower voice ABSENT FRIENDS and everyone else sa absent friends absent friends absent friends ect. and begin blubbing. In fact it do not seme that you can go far at xmas time without blubbing of some sort and when they listen to the wireless in the afternoon all about the lonely shepherd and the lighthousemen they are in floods of tears.

Still xmas is a good time with all those presents and good food and i hope it will never die out or at any rate not until i am grown up and hav to pay for it all. So ho skip and away the next thing we shall be taken to peter pan for a treat so brace up brace up.

The Molesworth Self-Adjusting Thank-You Letter

As an after xmas wheeze n. molesworth presents his self-adjusting thank-you letter.

Cut out hours of toil pen biting wear on elbows blotches and staring out of windows.

Strike Out words which do not apply.

Dear {
Aunt ....
Uncle........................
Stinker ....
Gran ....
Clot ....
Pen-Pal....................
}

Thank you very much for the {
train. tractor. germ gun. kite.
delicious present.* sweets.
space pistol. toy socks.
}

It was {
lovely. useful.
just as good as the other three.
not bad. super.
}

And I hav {
played with it constantly.
bust it already.
no patience with it.
given it to the poor boys.
dismantled it.
}

I am feeling {
very well.
very poorly.
lousy.
in tip-top form
sick.
} I hope you are too.

My birthday when next present is due is on................................

From..

(*Postage must be prepaid.*)

* When you can't remember what it was.

Welcome back for the new term,
molesworth! *Welcome Back!*